Grief, Your Way: Living With Loss

Health, hope and healing.

by Dr. Gabriel Constans

Grief, Your Way: Living With Loss
by Gabriel Constans, Ph.D.

JC Studio Press 2024
Ebook available.

CONTENTS

LOSS EFFECTS EVERY COMMUNITY

If you think that losses experienced by others or a book about death and grief are not your concern I'd ask you to think again. The cost, both individually and collectively, to our society of those experiencing complications from mourning is astronomical and all-encompassing.

Complex or *complicated mourning*, can be the result of multiple deaths, the death of a child, death from suicide, accident, homicide, unexpected loss and/or pre-existing conditions (before the death occurred) of alcoholism, abuse or mental illness. It is estimated that these difficult circumstances effect one out of every three mourners in the United States.

There are approximately 2 million deaths per year in the US alone. Each death, according to the research of Dr. Beverly Raphael, effects on average 8 to 10 family members (excluding friends, colleagues and other associations). Thus, a total of 16 to 20 million new mourners annually. With one in three of these mourners experiencing intense and complex mourning, the potential for 5 to 6 million instances of complicated mourning is very real.

The effects of grief, especially complicated grief, not only cause extensive individual suffering, but also bleed out into the workplace and community with increased drug and alcohol abuse among workers, absenteeism, accidents, ill-health, lower productivity and on occasion, social violence.

It is a natural instinct to deny, avoid or run away from pain. When someone in our life dies the emotion, thoughts and physical reactions can feel overwhelming and unbearable. To put it bluntly, it can feel like crawling through hell. And unless we recognize and acknowledge such feelings and find healthy ways to release the pain, the grief we experience comes out in unconscious ways and/or lies dormant until it is unexpectedly triggered by another event.

We aren't taught, nor do we have many examples of, how to "be" with feelings, thoughts or beliefs that make us feel uncomfortable and/or helpless. Instead of acknowledging such reactions in a safe environment or with someone we trust we tend to act out or numb out. Some of us do this by drinking and others by diving into increased use of licit or illicit drug use. Sometimes we work until we drop or stay active "doing something" to keep our mind off of the pain. At times we lash out and project our suffering on to others, inadvertently blaming everyone and everything outside ourselves for the pain we are experiencing within.

I believe and my experience has demonstrated that *the majority of the violence that exists and is perpetuated in the world, is the result of unrecognized and unresolved grief.* People act out their pain from loss on others.

What we do with our losses and the accompanying reactions of sadness, pain and grief, make all the difference in the world. In many respects the greatest gift we can give our families, communities and nation is to learn how to live with loss and pain without causing further harm to others or ourselves.

If you still don't believe another person's loss is any of your concern, I invite you to think about the deaths that have touched you, the web of lives that were and are effected by those deaths and gently reconsider.

UNIVERSAL AND EVER-PRESENT

Losses, separation, absence, decay and death follows us throughout our lives. There is no way to avoid change and the resulting grief and mourning that follow. This applies not only to the death of someone we love, but to all kinds of events and life circumstances, even ones that are initially experienced as joyous and happy occasions.

Weddings are loaded with unexpected losses. Even though they can be, "one of the happiest days of our lives", they can also be filled with fear, frustration and doubt. My wedding was wonderful, but it also had moments that I hadn't anticipated, like our honeymoon, which began with us both feeling sick from not eating any food and drinking too much wine during the celebration. So much for romance!

When you first meet someone and "fall in love", it feels wonderful. You may eventually decide to be friends and lovers, even life-long companions. But no matter how clearly and aware you are when you enter the relationship, it will change. You will discover things about one another that are annoying, that you don't like or didn't realize in the beginning and thus experience the loss of your previous perceptions. As time goes on one or the other gets caught up in work, tasks and goals and doesn't have the same energy or desire for expressing their love as they did before.

Every time something is not as we desired or expected, grief can creep up and smack us. Our parent doesn't say the things we want to hear. A friend says something hurtful. We don't get the job we want or we get the job we want and it is not what we had anticipated.

Having children, even with all its benefits and joys, contains constant change and loss. When I first become a father, the reality shattered my rosy-colored picture and expectations of parenthood. Along with the exquisite moments of love and connection, were the awesome responsibility and realization that this child would be part of my life forever. The time and attention they required was astronomical compared to what I had anticipated.

Your child is hurt, you don't like their teacher or they get sick and you grieve. Your child grows up and you grieve their lost innocence. They move out of the house or go away to college and you are surprised at how much you miss them, even though you knew it was coming and know it's "for the best."

Your friend leaves town, you move to a new house or apartment, you lose your job or a class or activity comes to an end. A movie or event doesn't match your expectations. You argue with your partner, friend or colleague. You separate or get a divorce from your mate – loss, loss and more loss.

We cannot stop the losses that are inherent in living, but I believe we can learn to live with them without letting them control our lives. Each time we pause and take a moment to acknowledge and identify each loss, we then have the choice of how or if, we choose to release the feelings, thoughts and fears they can generate. Once we do so, we can then bring ourselves back into the present and enjoy what is currently happening in our lives and look into the future.

When we recognize the impact that loss has on our lives, we can also choose to observe the opposite. For every loss, there is a gain and a new opportunity for growth and change. When a relationship, job or friendship changes, it can create other opportunities. It also gives us the chance to practice gratitude and recognize the things, people, situations and experiences that we DO have. The glass is not only half empty (loss), but also half full and we can choose what we wish to add next.

WHAT IS "NORMAL?"

Sometimes people ask right away. "Is this normal?" Others take their time, until they feel safe enough, then ask essentially the same question. "Am I going crazy?" "Do other people ever feel like this?" "Will I be OK?"

What they're referring to is the intense, overwhelming and often bewildering experience of the bereaved. The physical and mental reactions of shock, numbness, shortness of breath, racing heart, stomach upset, difficulty sleeping or eating, lethargy, exhaustion, forgetfulness, inability to focus, clumsiness and confusion, can all be part of the journey of loss. The emotional swings in mood from intense vigilance and anxiety to extreme pain, non-stop tears and sadness; are the body's natural response to the death of a loved one.

For many, whether you've had previous deaths in your life or not, it can be a frightening, bewildering and alienating experience. It feels like everything is hitting you at once and you aren't sure what to do next. Overnight, your entire world has changed. Life seems to be out of control.

Though grief and mourning are our bodies' natural reaction to separation, they can also resemble and/or mask symptoms of anxiety and depression. If, after some time, you are unable to function in daily life or are in doubt, do not hesitate to seek help, information and support.

More than likely, whatever you are experiencing is to be expected and there would be far more concern if you were not reacting at all. Having someone we love torn out of our physical presence or the thought of such a thing happening; can bring the strongest person in the world to their knees.

Feeling the full impact of loss, in some respects, seems to be the initiation fee we pay to be part of the human race.

HURRY UP AND SLOW DOWN!

"Summertime, and the living is easy..."

So sang Billie Holiday and Janis Joplin, among others. In reality, summertime wasn't always easy for them or for us.

Summer can be downright nasty and annoying. There are so many expectations and memories that we often feel flooded with thoughts of those not with us and/or overwhelmed in trying to fit a zillion plans into a short two-week vacation of intended leisure or relaxation.

For those who have had a loved one die, summer can not only be stressful but emotionally full of land mines. Memories of past outings, trips and visits to see friends and relatives can explode unexpectedly and knock us flat. Other reminders can creep up slowly, as we see a certain landmark, a sunset, hear a particular song on the car radio or see others with partners or family members who are now gone from our lives. It's easy to become jealous or melancholy without understanding why.

The stress of vacations can also deepen our sense of helplessness and pain by placing unrealistic expectations on what we can or can't do in a given amount of time. We generally try to hurry to get somewhere, so we can "relax" or see how many things we can accomplish, complete or stuff into a measly fourteen days.

We DO vacations like we DO bereavement in America. With most companies allowing but three days bereavement leave and two weeks vacation, per year, is it any wonder that our bodies contain and hold so much stress? We seem to believe that if we do something really quick and intensely, we'll power through whatever it is that's ailing us; such as grief or work. Never mind the fact that when someone dies our entire world can be turned upside down forever or that we spend more of our waking hours with those at work than we do with our partners or families. Yet, we seem to follow along with these expectations and take them lying down, or I should say while on the run.

A recent study of over a thousand men, over a ten year period, found that those who took more breaks and/or vacations had less mortality rates and/or fewer heart attacks or complications than those who didn't. What a surprise?!

Until we change the way we do business in this country or until we help create and insist on such changes, for the better health of all, there are a few things we can do.

Arrange more frequent breaks throughout the year, instead of taking all your accumulated time at once. Explore the possibility of working four or three day work - weeks (10-12 hours respectively), creating more time for you and your family.

Simplify. Look at the possibility of getting by with LESS stuff and having MORE time.

Be realistic. Don't try to cram a lifetime of desires into a two-week vacation. Always allow double the amount of time you expect to get to and from your destination. Think about what you wish to do with your time and balance it with what others want or expect of you. Enjoy the "getting there" as much as the arriving.

When you feel the summer pangs of sadness, jealousy or anger over a loved one's absence, remember to give your body and your heart a break. Don't expect yourself to be "over it" or to "forget about it." Like a good vacation, take the time to heal – eat, exercise, play, sleep - find healthy ways to grieve, validate your loss and RELAX.

"Your Daddy's rich, and your Ma's good-looking."

So goes another verse from SUMMERTIME. But having money or a pretty face doesn't lessen one iota of grief or create a better summer vacation. Life is short. Give yourself the gift of taking the time to taste it.

WHEN WILL THE PAIN STOP?

When you are feeling some of the most painful emotions you may have ever experienced, it is natural and understandable to want them to stop. One would have to be a masochist if they wanted such feelings to remain.

Thus, the understandable question, "When will it stop?!"

Unlike most kinds of pain however, which avoidance, medical attention or medication, can often remedy, the pains of grief are hard to shake, avoid or "get over."

If it was advantageous to avoid or medicate ourselves after a death, we would encourage everyone to do so, but usually such avoidance or use of chemicals to numb the body, heart and mind's reactions to separation, simply delay, suppress or complicate matters.

The pains we feel, when a loved one has died, do and can change, but not just with time. The old adage that "time heals all wounds" may be a comforting thought, but doesn't always pan out.

Learning how to honestly accept the reality of the loss, the changes it creates and the reactions that surface, in a safe, supportive environment (with or without others), tends to be one of the primary ingredients that can provide some relief, not just time.

Accepting the reality of the loss doesn't mean we like it or wish it had happened; but that we realize the person has died and aren't hiding from all the emotional impacts and changes that the loss has created.

Looking at our suffering honestly, not turning away, then

externalizing what we discover, without harming ourselves or others, takes some of the intensity and sting out of the journey of grief.

Many factors influence one's reactions to loss and the time it takes for the intensity and duration of pain to decrease. Some of these factors include the nature of the relationship, how you have reacted to previous crises, how the person died, your present support system and the familial, cultural and religious messages you've received about death, grief and loss.

No one can promise you a time when it will "be over", but with support, care and ongoing acknowledgement of grief's reality, the pain can lessen and change as we adjust to living life with the absence (as we physically knew them) of the person who died.

HERE TODAY – GONE TOMORROW

SUDDEN LOSS

There is no way to prepare. No way to brace yourself or let yourself down easily. When a loved one dies suddenly or their death is perceived as sudden, your entire world is turned upside down and inside out.

Luckily, our bodies have a built-in coping mechanism called shock. In a state of shock, we muddle through the fog of hearing what happened or remembering what happened, if we were there. We talk to people, go through the motions, attend the funeral, take care of matters that need attention and don't remember half of what we have done or not done. Life can seem like a dream. It's not real. There has been a mistake. It was someone else's husband, partner, friend, child or parent that died.

We may find our bodies feeling sluggish, exhausted, heavy, "not ourselves" and want to sleep, sleep, sleep.

While our body, mind and heart can feel like they're in a deep freeze, intermittent fears and worries about the future or "what will happen next", can cause us to be simultaneously on the alert (hyper-vigilant).

This mixture of feeling detached, numb and empty; combined with moments of intense apprehension and anxiety, are the double-whammy of sudden loss.

As the days pass and the numbness wears off or lessens (without another loss) all of these intense physical, mental and emotional reactions usually subside and decrease and the full impact and implications of the death on one's life start to come into full focus. That is when many are surprised to feel the depth of emotions and grief. "I was just starting to feel better." People say. "What's happening?"

We've just come out of the fog of shock and are suddenly confronted with feelings of anger, sadness, frustration and/or guilt. Our fears, anger and resentments start getting misdirected at surviving family members and friends or at ourselves. We burst out crying at the most inopportune times. We may try to "stay busy" or increase the use of other stimulants or substances to "get rid" of the pain, to suppress it.

If you have experienced a sudden death in your life, here are some healthy things you can do to care for yourself or another.

Upon notification **find a safe place** to be and surround yourself with people who will keep you going, give you food, call, stop by, remind you of daily needs, take you for a walk.

Eat one good meal a day. Exercise; even when you don't feel like it. **Rest and drink lots of water**, to counteract our body's dehydration during grief and sorrow. **Breathe**. Remember to consciously take deep breaths throughout the day and night.

Keep going. Don't give up. There IS a light at the end of the tunnel, even when you're in the depths of darkness. Life changes, feelings change, attitudes change, perceptions change and our understanding and appreciation of life are often awakened in the painful process of mourning.

Find a way to acknowledge and **release your pain in a safe manner**. Make it a daily habit, if even for only ten to twenty minutes. Try to pick the same time each day. During this time, talk or write to the person who died. Look at pictures. Go to their gravesite. Visit the spot where their ashes were scattered. Light a candle and/or some incense. Recall the past, events and memories. Say a prayer. Scream, yell, cry, wail, walk, run, chop wood, paint, make something, be creative. But, whatever you do during your daily ritual of remembrance, do it with the person who died in mind and in your heart. By taking the time, daily, to grieve the loss of the person who died (and all the ramifications of that loss), the moments that you lash out at others or try to hide from the pain, will tend to decrease. The overwhelming avalanche of emotions will diminish in frequency and intensity.

These suggestions and exercises do not make anything "go away" or stop the pain altogether, but they will take some of the constant sting off your daily life and leave you some room to breathe and catch your breath. Even though grief from sudden loss is symbiotic with feeling out of control, you can choose to let yourself be "out of control" in a safe, supportive environment and at a time of your choosing, to have more control over the rest of your life.

If sleeplessness, anxiety, depression or intrusive images persist, there are a variety of ways to obtain help. See your physician, or psychiatrist or contact a therapist.

CRY UNCLE! SUICIDE'S WAKE

"Yep, there's been lots of bears out here. Your dad and I almost got eaten alive once. Remember that Jerry?"

I was with my Uncle Danny and my father walking noisily along a woodland creek when he started in on one of his famous tales.

"Sure do." my Dad replied. "I thought we were dead meat."

"Come to think of it, it wasn't too far off from where we are now. We'd just walked around a blind corner of trees when out of the blue comes this nine-foot, growling grizzly. It stood straight up, roared and charged at us full speed!"

As I listened my feet began to feel like they were stuck in mud. I finally got them to move a few inches and strained my neck to see around the upcoming bend. He must have relished my increased apprehension as he continued his hair-raising story.

"Yep, it was scary alright."

Reluctantly I stuttered. "What happened Uncle Dan? How'd you get away?"

After a long pause and knowing glances between him and my father, he replied. "Luck Gabe, pure luck. We turned and tried to run, but your dad's so darned slow. The old grizzly was right at his heels, licking his chops! I picked up a rock about so big (he picked one off the ground the size of a baseball and displayed it as evidence), closed my eyes and threw it with all my might towards his gigantic jaws of death. The rock hit that crazed bear right between the eyes. It didn't really hurt him none, he was so big and all, but it stunned him just enough for us to scramble up the gully to our jeep and tear out of here."

"It was luck alright," my Dad interjected. "You throw about as good as you jive. You couldn't hit the side of a barn from five feet. I don't know how you managed to hit a marauding, man-eating bear from twenty paces. It's still hard for me to believe." He was grinning from ear to ear.

That was the first, but not the last time my uncle left me wondering which way was up. As I got older I learned that he was notorious for his inventive and intricate shenanigans, which he played on both family and foe. It may sound masochistic or foolish, but I'd be thrilled to have him pull the wool over my eyes again.

I always envisioned my uncle as a free-wheeling, fun-loving spirit, who made the most out of life. He had a beautiful, intelligent wife, Aunt Sharon; three bright, good-looking kids; was financially successful and enjoyed a variety of activities and pursuits.

Around this time of year, at one of my mother's early December birthday celebrations, Danny happily told my wife and I about their "wonderful" children and grandchildren and continually complimented us on our family and work.

Two weeks later my Dad called.

"Gate."

"Yeah."

"Did your sister call you yet?"

"No. Why?"

"Well... I've got some bad news."

"Are you OK?"

"Yeah. It's your uncle."

I couldn't for the life of me figure out what was going on.

"Danny?"

"Yeah." he stated flatly, followed by a long pregnant silence. I took a deep breath and asked, "What's happened?"

"Danny's dead."

"What!?"

"He killed himself."

"Come on quit joking around."

"I'm not kidding."

"When?"

"Yesterday. He shot himself."

"Oh, my God! Why?"

"He'd been depressed for a long time. I'm not surprised."

"Well, I am. Are you OK?"

"Yeah, I'm doing all right."

"How's Sharon and Mom?"

"They're hanging in there."

"I just saw him a couple weeks ago, he seemed fine."

"Well, he's had problems for a long time you know. He's told me several times over the last few years to not be shocked if I found him dead someday."

"Didn't he get any help or anything?"

"Oh yeah, he'd been doing everything. He was on medication for his depression, attended AA and saw a psychiatrist regularly."

"Depression. I didn't know he was depressed."

"Oh yeah. That's what's been eating him for so long. He just couldn't shake it. He tried everything."

"Man, I still can't believe it." I concluded.

Questions, questions, questions; my mind tried to bend around the unanswerable.

Three weeks after Danny's suicide I found myself crying at the drop of a hat, easily fatigued and having difficulty getting up in the morning. At first I couldn't figure it out. "I must have a flu bug or something," I'd tell myself. When the "flu bug" didn't go away after five days I told a friend and she pointed out the obvious. "Maybe the loss of your uncle's catching up with you."

Of course, she was right on the money. I'd been ignoring the obvious, like someone who thinks they've lost their glasses and they're right on their head. I slept in a little longer, took an extra couple days off work and let my tears fall whenever they came. My energy gradually returned, but I still felt like a dunce. "Why hadn't I known he was depressed?" Kept going around my brain. "If I'd known, maybe

I could have said or done something to stop it."

If I could talk to him now I'd remind him of the many lives he'd touched - for the better. I'd tell him his life has meaning and purpose. I'd tell him he's missed beyond comprehension. I'd let him know, in no uncertain terms, how much he'd loved and been loved by his family and friends. I'd tell him about this time my father and I were walking in the woods and were attacked by a giant grizzly!

DEATH AND THE WRITTEN WORD

How much information about dying, death and grief can we handle?

Jackie told me that after she was diagnosed with pancreatic cancer she was inundated with information, suggestions, advice and stories. She felt overwhelmed, confused and disoriented. Not only was she trying to make sense of the diagnosis and all its implications, she was also suddenly having to make decisions about what kind of treatment to choose, if any.

On top of such monumental choices, friends, relatives and health professionals bombarded her with written material on statistics, outcomes, recovery, remedies and self-help and self-care groups and organizations.

I asked her if she would rather not have all the information and she said, "No, I'd rather it was there than not. It isn't the information *per se*; it's how it is presented. I want it when I ask for it, not when others think I need it. I want to decide which things I wish to research for myself and which things I'd rather have someone else look into. I want to have some control over what comes my way and how I process it. There is enough out of control in my life as it is."

When I inquired as to how people would know when and how much to provide she replied, "Simply ask. All they have to do is ask and do so without judgment or 'should' attached to their question. Support offered when requested, without someone else's agenda attached, is the best medicine."

How may pamphlets, handouts, magazines and books can we read when we are taking care of a loved one who is dying or have just had someone die?

Brian took care of his wife (they'd been married for thirty-three years) for four and a half years until she died from complications of Alzheimer's eight months ago. He told me, "There were days when I could barely read the road signs, let alone an entire book. Taking care of Samantha took every ounce of energy and attention I could muster. One day a good friend of mine dropped off a little pamphlet about self-care. At first I didn't think much about it and just appreciated his show of concern. But every once in awhile I'd sit down, pick the thing up and read a sentence or two and try to do what it said. It wasn't anything monumental, but it helped me step back from my situation off and on and take a deep breath.

After Samantha died I tried to read a book or two again, but found I couldn't concentrate for more than a few minutes. I'd read the same sentence about three times before I realized what I'd just done. People gave me books about grief, but most of them were too big and intimidating. Again, it was this same friend who simply gave me a few handouts which had some common reactions and suggestions for coping with loss, which helped the most."

Do the words written on a page help us prepare any better for the inevitable or make the process of mourning any easier?

When Francis's mother was dying of congestive heart disease and came on to hospice services, the social worker gave her a handout that had information on a variety of topics (about hospice care, advanced directives, how to provide bodily care, etc.). It also included a page called "Signs of Approaching Death", which provided information on what physical changes "usually" happen as the body begins to shut down. Francis told me that the information helped her think about planning (both health care and financial) a little sooner than she might have otherwise and that the section on *Signs of Approaching Death* was especially helpful.

"Not long after I'd read that page, she started to decline." She explained. "If I hadn't known those things ahead of time it would have been VERY scary. As it was, I was able to relax a little bit and not freak out when her breathing changed and she began to slip away."

Francis echoed Brian's reactions about reading books on grief after her mother died and added, "I don't mind something more extensive, as long as I can keep it awhile and look at sections I need to, when I want to, then put it down and come back to it. The books have helped normalize my experience. They've let me know that many others have gone through what I'm going through and that I am not going crazy."

Twenty years ago there were only about twenty to thirty books available about death, dying and grief. There are now hundreds. The disadvantages to having so many are the difficulty in knowing which are right for you and your situation and which are not. The advantage is that there is far greater choice, they are more accessible and you are more likely to find something that speaks to you directly.

Like Jackie said, "When in doubt, ask?" Find out what kind of information they are seeking and how much they want at any given time.

If something you've read has deeply touched you, changed your life, or provided comfort, understanding or direction, the words will speak for themselves. You don't have to sell your experience or convince someone who is confronting illness, death or loss that the words you found so helpful will touch them in the same way.

SECONDARY LOSSES BECOME PRIMARY CONCERNS

Sometimes the more difficult losses are the ones that happen after our loved one is dead and buried. The additional loss (often referred to as "secondary loss") of having to move, leave friends, change jobs, schools and/or communities, can affect us as powerfully as death itself.

"I'm so sorry your father died. You must miss him terribly." A well-intentioned teacher tells a new student. "Yes." They reply. "But not as much as I miss my best friend Lisa and my old room."

When a child is asked such a question the answer is usually a simple "Yes" or nod of the head. It is not socially acceptable to say you miss your friend more than your father, so most people (adults included) keep their unacknowledged and private losses to themselves. They keep their unseen pain and resentments hidden under layers of protective shells and may or may not see them in themselves.

For many, it isn't that they disliked the person who died or didn't miss them terribly, but simply that other matters are presently taking priority. If the breadwinner in the family suddenly dies without having left any financial security for those left behind then they must deal with the changes that reality entails, focus their energy on the present crisis and struggle to survive. Their grief gets put on hold as their life is tossed upside down. We often tuck away the pain for the person who died until we have some stability in our lives, then become overwhelmed and surprised when the full impact of the loss hits us head-on.

"After my husband died from a heart attack." The mother of three stated. "I didn't know how we would get by. We didn't have enough money to make the monthly payments on the mortgage. My salary didn't cut it. I decided we had to sell the house and buy a small condo. We had lived in that house for sixteen years." She said sadly. "I tried to find a place in the same school district but they were all too expensive. I don't have any family in the area to help out and I refused to move back to the Midwest where my mother still lives. We ended up a way out of town. I had to change the two oldest kids to different schools and find a new daycare program for the youngest." Her eyes began to tear, as she looked down at the floor. "That was two years ago. It's only now that it's started to sink in, the fact that James won't be coming home. That he's dead. That I'm all alone."

Secondary losses can be difficult and complicated when you loved the person who died and just as painful and difficult when the person who died was someone you had mixed emotions about or even despised.

"I was shocked at the confusion and anger that bombarded me after my uncle killed himself." A man in his fifties told me. "He had always been such a bastard to my mother and I and I'm almost certain he abused my sister when she was little. I hated his guts and hadn't wanted anything to do with him." Pausing, his face turning red, he continued. "Then he goes and offs himself. Who had to clean up the physical and financial mess he left behind, my mother and me! Can you believe it? He's still screwing us over!"

Everyone experiences some secondary losses: some more than others. If a colleague, friend or family member has had someone die, don't automatically assume that all of his or her feelings are about missing the love and presence of the one who died. They may be feeling a mixture of complicated emotions and thoughts and may be more concerned with what's in front of their face than the one who is out of sight.

Don't be afraid to ask. Find out what is going on for them right *now*. Don't assume anything. Show your concern and care by asking honest, open-ended questions and acknowledging and validating their experience. Ask about other changes that may have occurred since the death. Ask them what kind of relationship they had with the person who died. Discover what kinds of support they have or don't have. What do they need? What do they want?

Leave your judgments and comments about where you think they should be or how they should be behaving in your mind's compost bin. You aren't them. You haven't had the *exact* same experience. You don't know the details or the intricacies of the relationship they had with the person who died. You don't have the right to walk their journey for them, but you can give them a lift to the corner store with some practical information, material assistance, listening ears and/or compassionate attention.

ON OUR OWN TERMS:

MAKING DECISIONS BEFORE IT'S TOO LATE

"Honey, we need to have a talk about sex." Your wife informs your daughter, after her birthday.

"It's time we discussed drugs and alcohol." You tell your son, before he goes to a party.

"You know you can talk to us about anything." You both say repeatedly to your children.

Then, one evening, your wife asks, "Have you ever talked to your parents about what they'd want us to do if something happened to them?"

"No." You say curtly. "I couldn't ask them that!"

"What if something happened to one of us?" She continues. "What would you want me to do? What would you do? What about the kids?"

"Stop being so morbid." You reply, annoyed that she's not dropping the subject. "Nothing's going to happen. We can talk about it later, OK?"

"But things DO happen." She persists.

"Please, just drop it." You reply, suddenly acting like you have to go do something.

Why has it become easier to talk about sex and drugs in our society, than it is to talk about death and dying? Why do we avoid the topic like the plague? What are we scared of?

The reality that our lives are limited, as well as those we love and that there will come a time when everyone we know, including ourselves, will die; causes a natural reaction of disbelief, numbing, avoidance and denial.

It's not that we don't see death; we're surrounded by it daily - in newspapers, TV, radio, magazines and the movies. But what we're surrounded by is not OUR reality. It is usually someone else, somewhere else, who is dying or has died by an accident, disease, homicide, disaster or suicide.

Death in the media is portrayed as sudden, quick and violent, or sudden, quick and peaceful. The reality of disease affecting us for months or years and/or the ongoing aftermath of loss are seldom portrayed or spoken of with any honesty or understanding.

Disease, injury, sickness and death are fundamental givens of life. What are we going to do about it?

As long as we keep silent, turn away or avoid these questions, we will continue to have little choice or control over dying without pain, dying at peace or preventing undue hardship and financial ruin on our families.

We don't have to wait until we are shocked into action. We can make choices now, on our own terms, without waiting to stare death in the face. Durable powers of attorney, funeral arrangements, long-term health care needs, resuscitation versus non-resuscitation, tube-feedings, discontinuing life-support, being a donor, preparing a will, writing down our wishes, can all give us more control and have things done on our own terms and not someone else's.

We may discover we have more to fear about not preparing for death, than we do with death itself.

SPEAKING WITH CHILDREN

Death can be scary enough as an adult, let alone as a child.

Imagine a pre-schooler whose grandfather has just died. He asks his mother what happened to Grandpa and is told "He died." A quizzical look crosses his face and he asks what "dying" means. His mother, not sure what to say, says quickly, "It's like sleeping or going on a long trip."

Is it any wonder that the child is afraid of going to bed that night or when one of his parents has to go out of town?

At seven years of age, a child's mother dies suddenly. Her father tries to explain what's happened and says, "God took Mommy to heaven to be with Him and Grandpa."

It should not be surprising when the child becomes angry with God for taking her mother and fearfully thinks, "If God can take Mom, how do I know they won't take Daddy too? Who's going to take care of me if Daddy's gone?"

When a friend's father dies of cancer, a teen's parents may say, "It's for the best. They were so sick," or "You've got to be strong for your friend."

The teen wonders how losing a father can "be for the best", doesn't feel "strong" and wonders what his parents would think if he ever became "so sick."

Euphemisms for death provide no comfort.

As a parent, relative, teacher or friend of a child who's facing death, here's what you can do to help.

Provide honest information appropriate to your child's developmental age. (Though there are exceptions, children under five generally do not comprehend that death is permanent. They can, however, feel the emotional atmosphere in their surroundings and respond to the reactions of significant others. Youngsters from age five to nine are better able to understand the meaning of physical death and that it is final. They may see death as "real", but not something that applies to them. Adolescents ten and older realize the full impact and painful reality of death, including the possibility of their own. To them death is a biological reality. The realization can affect their sense of safety and security.)

When asked what death means or where someone who died has gone, be true to yourself and your beliefs, but do so carefully, pay attention to the words you use and how they may be construed. Instead of saying "Grandpa went to sleep or is on a long trip." I've heard parents say, "Grandpa died. He will not be coming back. We'll always remember him and he'll always love you."

Reassure your child that their feelings are normal and provide outlets for them through physical activity, art, music, writing, etc.

Find support and take care of yourself to have to patience and clarity you need to give your child the same.

Let the child know you are willing to talk and LISTEN.

LISTEN to grieving children without trying to make it better or offering advice.

Notify the school and teacher of a death in the family and inform them of any concerns or changes.

Remember the "secondary losses" that result from a death, such as a change in caregivers, school or living environment, which can be equal to or more difficult an adjustment than the death itself.

If you feel your child is exhibiting an unusual behavior for an exceptionally long period of time, **seek help** from a qualified professional.

There is no magic formula for grieving and healing. You can only do the best that you can. Be gentle and forgiving with yourself and those around you. Everyone grieves in their own way and their own time... including the children we love.

HOLD ME CLOSE, BUT LET ME GO

MEMORIES

"Let them go."

"Get over it."

"Move on."

"Pull yourself together."

"Quit living in the past."

"Look towards the future."

"You must find closure and carry on."

Such common comments directed at the bereft send me up a wall and make me want to scream. And if it would do any good to scream at myself I would, because most of the time it's my own mind that's running these messages around in my head, bombarding me with what I should do. Sure, they're reinforced by family, friends and society, especially the media, but it is I who soak it up, repeat it like a mantra and then beat myself up for not getting "over it" (my grief) quick enough. But the reality is, at least my reality is that I *have* to remember. Remembering is the only thing that keeps me sane.

Remembering the dead is vital to our health. Keeping them with us, close to the bone, close to our hearts and minds, is the first step in transforming our past so we can bring them with us into the future.

Remembering *is* the road, the path and the catalyst that can teach us how to adjust to our loved one's physical absence and live a life that has room for them *and* those who are living.

Yet, as powerful as remembering can be, it is not enough to simply remember and tell our story. To bring those who have died into our lives and use their memory for our own good and the good of others, we must release the emotions that assault us when we are reminded of their absence.

When I look at the picture of our friend Marcia, who died in a car accident, I cry. When my eyes go to the next picture of my Uncle Danny, who killed himself, I cry. When I see my father-in-law, Claude, who was hijacked by Alzheimer's, I cry. Sometimes, in the midst of my tears, feelings of anger, guilt, frustration and helplessness crash land in my body. Once they are recognized, I cry some more and let them go.

In the past, during my morning ritual of remembering family members and friends, I often found myself grieving the loss of others as well; those who had been murdered, died in wars, starved to death, been crushed in earthquakes or swept away in floods. Since September 11th, I find I am crying for my uncle Danny and those at the World Trade Center, for our friend Marcia and those at the Pentagon, for my father-in-law Claude and those who perished in Pennsylvania. I am crying for their families, who have been thrown violently onto the gutted road of grief and mourning.

I hope I have enough room in my heart for *all* of those who have died and for those living. I hope I lead the kind of life that people who are gone no longer have the opportunity to live. I hope I can integrate death into life and use this precious container we call living to help others keep their loved ones present. I hope our world finds some meaning in the midst of such devastating losses and we discover how to remember, release and embrace our feelings of emptiness and helplessness with understanding, awareness and compassion.

I pray that we, as Americans, as citizens of the world, never forget those who have died, release the pain we feel with their absence and tenaciously hold on to them in any damn way we choose.

ALMOST HUMAN: PET LOSS

It is a fact of life that everything dies, including the animals we choose to care for. Dogs, cats, birds, fish and countless other living creatures all tend to have a shorter life span than humans, thereby increasing the chances that our beloved Labrador, tabby, parakeet or tetras will stop breathing long before we leave our mortal bodies.

To add insult to injury is the often callous or dismissive attitude and comments of others when we've lost a non-human friend. People don't always understand the emotional impact pet loss can have. They disregard our pain when we try to talk about the cat we've had for fifteen years getting sick and needing constant attention. They scoff at our tears, when our affectionate parakeet or terrier is lost or killed by a car.

They belittle our sense of shock and disbelief when the horse we've ridden, brushed, watered and cared for tenderly for the last eight years suddenly dies.

Yet, for some, pets, animals, and companions (whichever you prefer to use as a label for non-human creatures) are some of the closest and endearing connections we experience in life. Being responsible for any of the varied creatures placed in our care takes time, attention and devotion. And, just like people, such continued time and attention creates attachment, bonding and lasting imprints.

The love and commitment we give and receive from life's creatures is, in some respects, quite unique from that of other relationships. Sometimes, they are the only living beings that love us unconditionally and don't argue, judge or hurt us in any way. They also provide forms of communication beyond words. Their desire to be touched, patted, combed, and talked to provide warmth, softness, connection, meaning and continual reminders of enjoying the present moment.

A lady I recently met was shocked when told by her veterinarian that their beloved dog had cancer and should be euthanized. She refused and is currently seeking a vet that will give Hospice-type services for her dog and provide whatever is needed to make sure her family friend dies comfortably at home enjoying as many precious moments that remain. Like human beings, there should be an alternative for animals beyond that of further treatments or mercy killing.

Losing a pet also reawakens other losses we've experienced; whether recent or long ago. When a cat of ours, named Sushi, was killed by a dog a couple years ago, I unexpectedly found myself remembering my childhood collie, named Pinky and the grandmother I used to visit when Pinky was still alive.

The loss of an animal friend should be treated the same as that of a human. Talk about the loss; share your pictures, memories, tears and grief; have a service for your animal friend. Memorials and/ or funerals; provide validation of your relationship with that being; acknowledgement that there life was of value; and societal affirmation that all living creatures are to be honored and respected.

If you've lost a pet, at any time in your life and would like some additional support, outside your circle of family and friends, contact the SPCA (Society for the Prevention of Cruelty Against Animals), an empathetic therapist or your local grief-counseling center.

DEATH GATHERINGS:

HOW WE SAY GOODBYE

Gatherings for the dead have many names - funerals, memorials, remembrances, wakes, celebrations, send-offs and services, to name a few. They may be different in form, intent, content and cultural expectation, but they all speak to our human need to acknowledge the profound experience of death and make some sense out of loss.

Whether public or private, families, relatives and friends gathering to proclaim the life and death of someone they know, is a centuries-old ritual that can provide comfort, solace and support. And though it is usually a painful occasion, by stating out loud and with others that the person has died, it can also be the catalyst for survivors to accept the reality of the death and begin to absorb all the implications it has for their lives.

It is difficult to continue living if we do not stop and acknowledge the feelings, thoughts and reactions that occur when death has hit home. It is difficult, if not impossible, to continue living, if we don't recognize the dying. Funerals give us the opportunity to say, "Yes, my loved one has died. Yes, other people recognize the fact of their death. I am not alone in this experience. In the midst of death, there are the living and the memory of the one who died. Yes, I see that their life has had an impact on others as well as myself. Their life was significant. Their existence in my life had and will continue to have meaning."

It can be a room with hundreds of mourners telling stories about the deceased or a small family gathering of two, spreading the ashes (remains) together at sea. The act of remembering, acknowledging and validating the life of the one who has died and those who remain is vital for our health. Some would say that how we treat the dead is a good indication of how our society treats the living.

Over the years, I have attended hundreds of services. Even though they are not always what every surviving family member envisions, nor are they always what the deceased said they had wanted, every service had some value and meaning for those who attended. Yes, people judged one another at many services on how this or that person should or shouldn't act and some services displayed the conflict between family members rather than their bonds. Yet, every service made the fact of the death undeniable, the reality of the change obvious and the opportunity to see the limitations of our relatively short lives and re-evaluate our values, priorities, beliefs and commitments.

A friend of mine told me she had reluctantly gone to her stepfather's open-casket funeral (where you see the person who has died). She had initially dreaded the idea, but found, to her surprise, that the experience helped her become less afraid of death. It was different than what she had imagined when hearing of his death by phone. She said it also gave her time to reflect on her stepfather's life and how he influenced, both negatively and positively, her own and that of her siblings.

Nobody (child or adult) should be forced to attend, view or take part in a gathering to honor the dead. You can encourage people to attend, educate them on its significance and what to expect. Support them before, during and after the event, but never force or insist upon their presence.

Some of us, due to distance, finances or family dynamics, never get the opportunity to attend a memorial or service. That doesn't mean that we cannot create our own service or ritual in some way, at some time, that fulfills our need to publicly and/or privately say goodbye. You might consider putting an add that remembers your loved one in the local paper. Invite some personal friends to your own gathering. Create a work of art (painting, poem, sculpture, garden, etc.). Make a collage, video or scrapbook of photos of the one who has died and/or write an essay about their life and share it with others. Volunteer, do some work or live your life in a way that honors and remembers the deceased.

Whether we attend a gathering to honor the dead in person or create our own, the ritual, in fact the very act and process of creating the ritual, can often provide greater understanding, a profound release and an ongoing connection with the one who has died.

DOES DEATH CHANGE OUR SPIRITUAL BELIEFS?

I wish death happened like it used to in the old Hollywood movies. You know, those deathbed scenes where everyone gathers around, makes amends, says their goodbyes and drift off with visions of God and the angels dancing in their eyes. But it rarely does. Deathbed conversions are few and far between.

When death approaches or has taken place, most people live their faith, their beliefs (or their disbelief) in a God or the hereafter the same as they have the rest of their lives. If they believe in some creative force that is more than what we can see, they continue to do so through sickness and loss. If they believe God has a plan for everything that happens and that Jesus is their savior, they continue to do so until their dying breath. If someone feels that there is no God, supreme being or spiritual meaning for anything on earth, they hold on to that belief even after their loved one's body is buried deep in the ground.

A friend once told me, as their mother was dying, that no matter how hard she tried she couldn't make herself believe the same as her mother had all her life. She desperately wished she could. She wanted to understand and connect with her mother before she passed on in a way she had never been able to. She said that for a while she pretended to believe as her mother had, but she knew she was pretending. She even went to her mother's church and read the same readings and scriptures, without any change of heart.

A client I met with for several months repeatedly expressed her frustration that her husband had never believed in God and she couldn't understand how he had gone to his death without accepting God into his life. For over forty years she had tried to convert him and get him to go to church, always believing that someday he would see the spiritual light.

A member of my family had an understandably difficult time when my uncle killed himself and sincerely worried about his soul, wondering if he was suffering as much after death as he had during life. They prayed that God would forgive my uncle and provide the serenity that had always seemed to be just beyond his reach. The only way they could make sense of the tragedy was to believe that he was "in a better place." They had always believed that God provides happiness and peace and used that faith to provide personal comfort, safety and meaning.

Belief in God, a Great Spirit, Nature, Jesus or some other religion or spiritual path, doesn't mean that people don't question, argue, bargain or get angry with that in which they believe.

A colleague of mine was enraged when her daughter was killed in a car accident. She felt like her religious tradition had lied to her. "How could a loving God let such a bad thing happen to such an innocent child?! How could He take her at such a young age?!" She still believed in God, but couldn't make sense of what had happened. "Somebody was responsible for this!" She said. "There has to be a reason!" She prayed to God for an answer. "But all I could hear was myself talking to the empty air." She explained. "It took me years of asking 'why', begging for an answer, before God gave me the strength and understanding to live with not knowing."

Another client blamed God for allowing her abusive ex-husband to survive and live with his alcoholism, while her hard-working, kind friend died from liver cancer. She overflowed with unanswerable questions. "Why didn't that son-of-a-you-know-what get this awful disease instead? Why does my friend have to deal with this? What did she ever do? Why? Why? Why?" Her friend continued to work as long as possible and remained true to her sweet loving self until her death a year and a half later.

As in most sweeping statements of finality, there are exceptions. Occasionally someone reacts to death and loss differently than they have lived the rest of their lives.

A woman I interviewed a few years ago said she made a bargain with God and it changed her life. As the car she was driving hit a side rail on the freeway and began rolling over and over she said, "God. If you let me live to raise my young son I'll dedicate my life to you." She had never believed in God and didn't know where that had come from, but she said she heard a voice answer her that said, "Yes." She survived the accident, continued raising her son as a single parent and never forgot her promise. Though she had always seen herself as a selfish person she started thinking of others and became involved in several charities. When her son was killed ten years later she never wavered from her promise and used her son's death to inspire her to do even more of "God's work."

Death and grief can crack open our hearts. They can change our perceptions of how we see the world. They can wake us up to the reality of pain and suffering in ways that we never thought possible. Within the midst of such grief and pain we can reach out for comfort, look within for guidance and find compassion and forgiveness from our religion, community or sense of personal responsibility.

Mourning can be a catalyst for clarifying our values and deepening our understanding, but it doesn't mean we will throw our beliefs out the window or change our spiritual faith. We need not despair over our usual conditioned human response to loss. There's always an old Bette Davis movie with a good deathbed scene we can find at the video store, take home and imagine ourselves saying our good-byes, making last minute amends and being carried off to the heavens!

MEMORIAL DAY

PERISHED AND PRESENT

Memorial Day – "a legal holiday in the U.S. in memory of the dead servicemen of all wars." That's how Webster's defines Memorial Day, but is that what takes place? Has this day of remembrance become just another holiday; another three-day weekend; a day of forgetting?

Memorial Day can be a powerful reminder and opportunity for honoring and remembering our dead; for paying homage to those who died believing that their lives made a difference; and that their lives were sacrificed for the benefit of others.

In many respects, those who have died for this experiment in democracy are still living. They're living in the water we drink, the food we grow, the ballot we cast, the policies we protest, the pains, sorrows and struggles of everyday life.

I respect the men and women who fought to end slavery in the Civil War and those, like my grandfather William, who fought in World War I, believing it would be "the war to end all wars." I remember and give thanks to my father-in-law, who fought during World War II against the Nazis and lost his parents, grandparents, family and friends in the concentration camps. I thank my friend's father, Charles, who froze to death in Korea to stop, what he thought at the time, was another fascist plague. And I remember and honor all those who died in Lebanon, Panama, Somalia, the Persian Gulf and Viet Nam, as well as those who returned from those conflicts and died from resulting disease, addiction or suicide.

Though Memorial Day honors those who have died during wartime, let us not forget the military women and men who have died outside of conflict; those who have died while training; while in transport; during missions of peace and rescue; and at home from illness, accident, governmental disregard or neglect.

Before we can ever proclaim, "Never again!" we must exclaim, "Never forget!"

Never forget the soldiers and civilians who have perished. Let us honor their memory, by keeping them in our hearts and doing everything possible to prevent and end the wars that have caused such great sorrow and suffering. Take some time to bring out pictures, tell stories, make a toast, thank those still living and recommit ourselves to the peaceful resolution of conflict.

Memorial Day reminds us that blood and tears are the same in any language. Every life is precious and every loss must be remembered, mourned and honored.

LIVING WITH THE DEAD

They're all around us – in the rooms we walked through day after day, year after year; working in the garage with their tools; in the kitchen baking, talking, preparing a holiday meal; and in our beds at night. We can almost see them, feel them; hear them breathing in their sleep. Our dead children, fathers, mothers, grandparents and lovers have left us physically, but stay imprinted in objects, memories, special occasions and our minds and hearts.

We can't really forget them, not even when we try and at times we try REALLY HARD. Sometimes we stay busy, busy, busy and work, work, work. At other times, some of us drink, use drugs or go to physical and emotional extremes, anything to try to forget the memories and pain of our losses. As a result, we not only still think about and miss those who have died but then have the additional complications of physical deterioration or addiction. It turns out we've been running the wrong way.

What we need most often is to remember and decide how we want to keep those who have died present, not absent. What do we remember and miss about them the most? What aspects of their lives had the greatest influence on ours? Which of their actions or behaviors do we want to leave behind and not continue? How did their life and our knowing them shape who we have become? What feelings and thoughts do we want to hold on to and embrace? How can we acknowledge and grieve the loss of those who have died before us, adjust to life without them physically visible and still stay connected with them in our daily lives?

Dia de los muertos (Day of the Dead) is one, powerful Mexican tradition that can help those of us still living to honor and integrate those who have died into our daily lives. The Day of the Dead invites family members to visit the sites where their loved ones are buried, to offer them food and flowers, display pictures, light candles and talk about the family, the pain of the deceased's absence and life's ongoing joys and sorrows. It's a celebration of those who have died and a way for those living to remember.

Most cultures in the world have similar traditions and exercises to help them remember. Many Asian, African, Native American and European communities have altars in the home that consist of pictures of the dead (or items that represent them) and frequently light incense or candles and speak to or say prayers for, those who have died.

The reason millions of people throughout the world continue to practice these rituals, century after century, is because they work! They provide comfort, solace, meaning, understanding and connection in a safe, familiar and accepted way.

Of course you need not wait for just one special day of the year to remember, honor and memorialize your loved one. You can make it a daily practice. Even if it's only for five to ten minutes, take a moment to speak with, think about, write to, look at or create something for, your loved one who has died. Do it in a place that is special for you – your favorite corner of a room, somewhere in your garden, by the beach, in the redwoods, at the graveside or with someone you trust. There is no right way to do it (as long as it doesn't harm yourself or others) and you will surely find aspects of your remembrance that are unique to you and your loss.

A private, daily celebration of the Day of the Dead has the wonderful side effects of lessening the intensity and frequency of grief's pain, as well as nurturing a realistic, ongoing relationship with those who have died. How we treat the dead can also reflect and/or mirrors how we choose to stay connected too and relate with, those who are living.

THE WRONG KIND OF DEATH

WHEN SOCIETY IGNORES OR JUDGES OUR REACTIONS

"What are you so upset about? It was only your ex-husband."

"Come on, get over it. You can always get another cat."

"Hey, you hadn't seen your friend in years anyway."

"They were drunk half the time. Who cares?"

"It's not the same as being married. You just lived together."

"You only knew them for two months!"

"Weren't they old? They lived a long life."

"No, you can't come to the funeral. You aren't part of the family."

These are just some of the comments that people hear and a small sampling of how their grief is disregarded after they've had a friend, acquaintance or family member die. The losses they have experienced don't match the images of who and what is acceptable to grieve in our society. And it's not just others that cause such pain. We are often our harshest critics.

We internalize the conscious and unconscious messages we are fed daily and are often confused with the intensity of our emotions and reactions after a death, when our head is telling us we should not be feeling much at all.

Our response to any kind of loss, especially from death, is our bodies natural reaction to the human condition, even though we analyze it, distrust it and, at times, find it hard to believe.

"Why am I getting so upset over my ex-husband's death? We never got along and I've been better off without him."

No matter what the relationship was like, it was a relationship. There were attachments, habits and shared time that will always effect one's life. For some, the never-ending hope of reconciliation will have died as well.

"It was only a cat. I know it's not the same as a person."

Your cat or pet was a living creature. We can grow just as accustomed and fond of an animal as we can with a human. The same kind of attachments and memories occur.

"We were best friends during high school, but that was ages ago."

Some friends stay with us forever, whether we see them often or rarely at all. The time we spend together can leave us with lasting imprints, influences and memories, as well as regrets, bitterness or pain.

"This is crazy. His drinking ruined our family and our lives. He was mean and abusive. Why is his death so hard? I thought I'd be relieved."

Even abusive, negative relationships can cause unexpected mixtures of emotion. Though we may have separated ourselves from the individual and learned how to fend for ourselves or are still in contact, there is usually some deep feelings of loss over the years they were not the parent or partner we had wished for. The realization that they have died can also awaken the fact that the opportunity for them to change or be different has died as well.

"We were only housemates. It wasn't like we were married or anything."

Whether as a friend, lover, roommate or relative, living in the same household is one of the most intense experiences in our lives. It's where we learn how to interact with others and provides daily reminders of our differences and similarities. Whether two people living in the same household have their arrangement sanctioned or accepted by others does nothing to diminish the powerful lessons and connections that develop. We are intimately shaped; both good and bad, by those with whom we live.

"I just met them two months ago, but I can't stop thinking about them."

The length or duration of a relationship doesn't necessarily mean that it is of greater or lesser importance or impact. Some people we've known for years, yet have little connection, do not effect us deeply upon their passing, whereas others we've just met leave lasting footprints. The grief and mourning that result from the loss of a recent or longtime acquaintance is VERY individual and unique to that person, as are our needs in grieving their loss.

"Grandma was eighty-five years old. I knew she wouldn't last forever, but it feels so sudden. I loved her so much."

The longer someone you know lives, the harder it can be to accept the reality of their death. Even though you may have had time to prepare and say and do what you needed or wanted to, it can still seem like it came too soon. There are times when no matter the person's age, you want them to stay forever and their death is devastating.

"They never accepted me. I should have known this would happen."

You have a right and a human need to attend the funeral and/ or memorial of your partner. Your relationship with the deceased was between you and them, not their family or friends. How your relationship was seen or accepted by others is important in your adjusting to the loss, but not dependent upon it.

There are times when those you expect to be of help are not always able or willing to do so. For some, it is too painful. Others find it impossible to stop judging long enough to listen. When you can't attend the funeral or memorial, due to the deceased's family, distance or other circumstances, create your own ritual or ceremony of leave-taking. Invite those who will be present to you and share your loss.

Relationships with people and other living creatures are what make us human. It is normal to question, criticize and judge our selves after someone in our life has died. It is also normal to feel pain, frustration, anger, sadness, relief and confusion.

If you don't get the kind of support and acknowledgment you need from family, friends or colleagues, then find it elsewhere. Don't minimize, trivialize or try to forget your loss. Find ways to acknowledge, respect, honor and validate your experience and the reactions that have resulted.

WHAT DID YOU SAY?!

WHEN LIFE CHANGING ILLNESS WALKS IN THE DOOR

It felt like I had been hit by lightning.

"Gabriel." My sister Candace said, with a voice that was close to breaking. "I have breast cancer."

After a moment of stunned silence, not sure I had heard her right, I said something stupid like, "Are you sure?"

"They're doing a lumpectomy and then they're talking about radiation, chemotherapy and hormone treatments." She continued, while I sat numb, listening on the phone to the litany of assaults upon her body that she was about to begin.

"Do you have to have all the other stuff after surgery?" I wondered out loud. "If it's all in one area and they remove it all, why do you have to still do everything else?"

"Just to make sure." She replied. "The other therapies make it less likely that it will ever reappear and since I'm so young, with children, they don't want to take any chances." She paused and swallowed. "And neither do I."

I still couldn't believe what I was hearing. My little sister, the only biologically related sister I have (the other eight being foster sisters) and the one I've known since her birth, two years after mine, just told me she had a disease that she could die from. And, because I have worked at a hospice for many years, with people living the last months and days of their lives due to cancer and other diseases, my first reaction was that she was going to die.

As if she was reading my mind she said, "The odds are really good that it will all work out fine, but I wanted to let you know."

She was right, the odds for full recovery from early-detected breast cancer are very good and have continually improved over the last ten years, but knowing that fact didn't help much when I was used to seeing or hearing all about those who hadn't survived.

"Have they told you about all the side effects?" I asked, aware that, at least in the past, physicians and nurses sometimes minimized the amount of discomfort and reactions that can occur from chemotherapy, radiation and hormonal therapies.

"Yeah." She said. "They told me about all the worst things that could happen. They said they had to tell me, even though none of them would probably occur."

"Sure." I thought. "I've heard that before, then seen people get as sick and tired as an old dog and feel like the treatment was killing them worse than the cancer." But, I couldn't tell my sister that. At least I didn't think I could at the time. I wanted to be hopeful and supportive so I said, "Good. I'm sure you'll do real well."

She went on to describe when, how and what would happen and how she had discovered the lump. She said that in some ways it was a relief to at least know what it was and why she had been feeling so uncomfortable in that area.

I asked the usual questions. "Do you want me to come up and help with the kids? Is there anything I can DO?"

"No." She replied. "I'm OK. Mark (my brother-in-law) will

watch the kids and Mom and Dad and other friends are all going to pitch in. The people at work told me to take as much time as I needed."

Being told that you or someone you love has a life-threatening illness seems to bring up two strong, common reactions. One is anxiety. "What will happen next? Will they or I, be OK? How will it affect this or that? How long will this last? Will they or I die?"

The other reaction, that can happen after some time has passed from the initial diagnosis or occasionally, almost immediately, is "What is really important to me? What are our priorities in life? What do I REALLY care about most? I'll never take anything for granted again. How will this illness effect the rest of my life and how will I live the life I have?"

My first reaction to Candace's news was intense anxiety and fear. After her surgery had passed and treatments began, I started to look at our relationship, find some meaning in what was happening and appreciate the closeness we have. Her reaction, from what she told me, was much the same.

If there is any blessing or "hidden golden lining" in confronting and living through or dying with a life-threatening illness, it must be the sense of presence and appreciation it can give us for the short lives we are living. It makes our mortality real and thus provides a container for the preciousness and value of every life.

Before Candace was diagnosed with cancer, she would have been the last person in the world to ever seek counseling or attend a support group. I don't know if that was because our mother had always tried to get her to do so as she was growing up and/or because it was something I have always been involved in. But, after her surgery, she started seeing a private therapist and then attended a cancer support group. I was really taken aback when she first told me she was utilizing such support.

As the months went along, Candace told me of the insights and changes that counseling and the group were creating within her and how she was realizing that she has far more choice in how she chooses to live her life than she had previously envisioned.

I guess that's what people mean when they say that having cancer was or is a blessing, because it helped them to "wake up" and live life instead of being a victim of life.

Luckily, after about two years, Candace is done with all her treatments; and free and clear of any signs of cancer. I think she sees life differently now and has a deeper awareness, understanding and compassion for others. She's not as afraid of sickness and death as she had been and thus can help others who are confronting the same thing.

I wish there were a switch we could turn on when we hear bad news, a switch that takes us immediately to hope meaning and compassion. But, more often than not, anxiety, fear and apprehension are first to take us on the roller-coaster ride of grief.

If I can remember when hearing bad news that feeling anxiety, fear and helplessness is normal, expected and understandable; perhaps I'll be better able to acknowledge those reactions more quickly and use the information as a teacher for clarifying my values instead of a doomsayer predicting a horrifying future.

CAN WE LAUGH ABOUT IT?

A famous comedian once said that "Life is a sexually transmitted terminal disease." And as far as I know, it still happens to ten out of ten of us. So, is it OK to laugh about this solemn reality? Is it OK to poke a little fun at the Grim Reaper and not offend or upset anybody? I think so. In fact, I believe we can step back and take a lighter look at death, dying and grief that can, on occasion, help us get through some of the most painful moments in our lives.

I recall an incident many years ago when a family and I were all keeping a bedside vigil with a woman in her seventies, who we'll call Martha. Martha was going in and out of consciousness and talking out loud to and about people we couldn't see.

One evening she kept looking up by the ceiling in one corner of the room and saying, "The light. The light."

Her daughter replied, "Yes, Mama. Go towards the light."

Martha became more agitated and repeated, "The light. The light."

We all smiled, believing she was speaking about the light at the end of the tunnel that some people describe in near-death experiences. I said, "Yes, Martha. It's OK. Go towards the light."

Finally, out of total desperation, Martha forced herself to sit up. She opened her eyes, pointed at the corner of the room and said, "The light bulb. It needs a new light bulb." Then she lay back down and continued her dialogue with family members who had already died.

Embarrassingly, we all realized that she had been talking about the lamp in the corner all along. I went to check it and discovered that it did indeed need a new light bulb.

A woman whose husband of thirty years had died just six months previous to our meeting had been talking for quite some time about the deep pain and sadness that had enveloped her since his death when she suddenly burst out laughing.

She laughed uncontrollably for a few minutes and after blowing her nose and wiping her face said, "He could be the biggest pain in the butt when it came to doing the dishes. If he ever did them at all, I had to do them again. His idea of clean wouldn't have passed muster at the city dump." She grinned. "He'd die laughing if he saw the sink now. I haven't done the plates or silverware in a week. The food's so caked on it will probably take a chisel to get it off." She paused, then said, "I never thought I'd miss his dirty dishes."

Then there was Cliff, a retired schoolteacher. Cliff told me this story about his deceased friend Barney with a very somber, straight face.

"You know." He said. "Barney and I were best friends for over thirty years. I remember a couple of times before he died when we talked about reincarnation and all that stuff. Neither of us has ever been very religious and didn't think much about it, but we agreed that if it was real, that whoever died first would come back and let the other know what it was like."

Cliff paused, to make sure he had my attention.

"Well," he continued. "After Barney passed on I went to the same little bench on West Cliff Drive where he and I used to sit and shoot the breeze for hours. You know, that one by the lighthouse?" I nodded. "I went there every day and waited, just in case, by some fluke, this reincarnation thing was legit. Well, wouldn't you know it, last Saturday I was sitting on our bench when I heard someone whisper, 'Cliff. Cliff.'"

I sat back a little and raised my eyebrows at Cliff, with some suspicion, but he continued with so much sincerity that I couldn't dismiss it altogether.

"I'm not making this up." He said adamantly. "So, I look around and don't see anybody. Then I here it again."

'Cliff. It's me, Barney.'

"Barney?" I says. "Is that really you?"

'Yep.'

"Well I'll be." I exclaimed. "Where are you? I can't see you."

'Naw.' Barney replied. 'They let me come like this for a little bit to let you know what's up with this reincarnation thing.'

"What do you mean?" I said.

'Well, it's the funniest thing.' Barney explained. 'All I do nowadays is sleep, make love and eat.'

"What?" I said.

'Yeah. That's all we do.' Barney reiterated. 'Sleep, eat, make love, go back to sleep, then wake up and do it all over again.'

"Well, I finally had enough of this nonsense," Cliff explained, "so I asked him straight out, "So, old friend. Who are you now and where are you?"

"And you know what he says?" I shook my head no. "He says, 'I'm a rabbit on a breeding ranch in Idaho.'"

I'd been had by one of the best. Cliff and I both chuckled over his story. He said it felt good to be able to laugh. "Barney and I used to say, if you can't laugh at yourself now and then, then you're taking life much too seriously."

Cliff was on to something. It shows no disrespect towards those who have died to have a good laugh, even if it relates to them. Most deceased friends and family would want nothing more than our happiness if they were still here to tell us so. As the centurion George Burns used to say, "If I look in the morning paper at the obits and see that my name isn't there, I know it's a good day."

WALKING WITH ANXIETY AND FEAR

Even though anxiety, fear and terror are a reality most people live with, in varying degrees, we do not have to let these feelings control, manipulate or ruin our lives.

Pain and loss or the thought of future pain and loss can at times feel like an unbearable burden. Waiting for the next shoe to drop or wondering when the shoe that already dropped will ever go away, is a normal human reaction to the discomfort and weight of anxiety. Questioning whether such intense apprehension and fear will subside can keep our bodies and minds on ever-vigilant overload and cause numerous physical emotional and mental difficulties.

Numerous factors can contribute to or create anxiety. Some are obvious: the sudden or expected death of a loved one, friend or colleague; the loss of a relationship; an act or threat of terrorism; divorce or separation; sexual and/or physical abuse; changing, losing or starting a new job; and moving to a different part of town, the nation or another country. Less blatant, but potentially as nerve-racking, are the pace of our society constantly moving faster; our diet and the foods we eat and how quickly we eat them; and the sadness and helplessness that can arise when we acknowledge the inequality and suffering in the world and the possibility that all life on earth is in jeopardy.

I remember jumping at loud noises for several months after my friend died in a car wreck. I also found myself excessively worrying about something happening to members of my family and thinking that I could be next every time I got behind the wheel. I had difficulty sleeping, which decreased the amount of energy and awareness I had the rest of the day and made me irritable and bossy with others in order to have some sense of control and stability.

What a relief when I recognized what was happening and that I wasn't alone. According to the Anxiety Disorders Association of America, "anxiety is now the most commonly diagnosed mental illness in the country" and one of the least treated. It is estimated that only about 25% of adults experiencing mild to severe forms of anxiety seek or receive any treatment for it.

Luckily, there are means and ways to decrease, relieve or transform anxiety, panic and fear.

The first step and perhaps most important, is to acknowledge, admit or identify when or if you are anxious, scared or fearful, though this isn't always as easy as it sounds. Sometimes we have been anxious for so long we can't see it for what it is and point the finger at someone or something outside ourselves. It can also be clumped together with depression, anger, sadness, guilt, etc. Once we can see it for what it is, we can then choose to take some constructive action.

One of the first actions we can take is to consciously "take a deep breath." Yes, it's an old cliché, but it turns out to have some merit, especially in relation to anxiety. A study in the *Journal of the American Medical Association* found that slow diaphragmatic breathing (similar to Yoga breathing practices) was just as effective in reducing anxiety as an antidepressant drug.

Some people find that medication, carefully monitored for side effects with their doctor, is a valuable and efficient tool to eliminate panic attacks and chronic anxiety. They can be helpful for months or years, depending on each individual's tolerance and reactions.

Cognitive or Talk Therapy (in which triggers that create anxiety are identified, reduced or re-directed) has helped some people reduce, if not eliminate, many of their fears and phobias.

There is also a technique called Thought Form Therapy that involves identifying what it is that one is fearful or anxious about, either remembering the feeling from a previous event or at the time it is happening and tapping on specific points on the body. These points correspond with the meridians used in Acupressure. Like deep breathing, this seems very simple, yet research and clinical practice have consistently found it to be effective in eliminating anxiety and nightmares.

Several studies, including one in *The American Journal of Psychiatry*, have concluded that mindfulness meditation effectively reduces panic and anxiety symptoms. Mindfulness meditation combines breath and awareness to notice what we are experiencing moment to moment and learning how to neither push our thoughts, feelings and sensations away or hold on to them.

The famous presidential quote from the 1930's that, "We have nothing to fear but fear itself", doesn't adequately portray all of life's realities. There are countless things to fear besides fear itself, but when anxiety, apprehension and fear control our lives it can seem like it is all that exists.

Don't run away from fear and anxiety. Look it straight in the eye and find what works best to put it in context with the rest of your life so you can experience some peace, serenity, joy and hope.

WHEN A WOMAN MOURNS

"Emotional, tearful, talkative, weak, dependent, scattered, illogical, over-reacting, out of control and hysterical." These are some of the judgments and labels that women are painted with when they react to the loss of a loved one.

Sometimes women (and men) do react to a sudden or expected death with a great deal of emotion and cry, talk, scream, wail and/or moan. Thank God that they do, for by doing so they are teachers for both sexes of how to honor and acknowledge a natural, human response to loss.

If people are not allowed to "let go", "collapse" or "lose it" after the death of a loved one, when on earth can they? When is there ever a better time to release the anguish and pain of having someone or a number of people ripped out of your life?

There is nothing inherently "weak" in allowing the true depths of our suffering to surface. It takes a lot of strength to allow oneself to be so vulnerable and honest. It takes incredible energy, support and awareness to do something that most Americans have pathologized, minimized or tried at all costs to "get over."

Yet, more often than not, women are the pioneers in taking this journey of mourning, of walking through the valley, stepping on the sharp rocks and finding their way back to life; often with a newfound respect and appreciation the preciousness of life.

In some cultures, both here and abroad, some women are the "designated mourners" at funerals and are the ones who show up at families' homes when there has been a death. They hold a place of honor in their communities, because of their ability to connect with, hold and release the individual and the communal pain of loss and separation that has occurred. Like midwives at births, these women are held in high esteem, as strong, aware healers who have their feet planted solidly on the earth, while their hearts compassionately open to both the suffering and the pain.

We, as a society, have slowly begun to recognize the power of grief and mourning and are starting to realize that such reactions are normal, for both women and men and that to not have such outward or visible reactions to loss is also an acceptable way to mourn.

Because of past conditioning by families, institutions and media, women have often bought into the stereotypes of how they should or shouldn't grieve and mourn. If they aren't crying, sad, depressed or screaming after the death of a loved one, they often think something is wrong, that they're "weird" or "abnormal."

Just as there is a wide variance in men, with regards to how we react, process and think about loss, so to for women. There are no universal women or universal men with exact, programmed responses to life and death. There are countless ways in which we mourn.

How we react to loss is the outcome of hundreds of factors, including, but not limited to, our relationship with the deceased; how long we've known them; how we have dealt with past crises; how old we are; how they died; whether we were with them or not at the time of death; how we were told of their death; what kind of support system we have or don't have; other responsibilities; financial or health concerns; what our belief systems are; and the messages we have received from others on what is or is not acceptable.

I have met women who were in great turmoil because they were not proceeding as "planned" by their and/or others' expectations of when, how and where they should be at a given time, in regards to their grieving or reactions to the loss of a loved one.

One woman had not cried since the death of her father six months previous. She thought something was "wrong" with her. Yet, after describing everything she had had to do in the last six months and the kind of relationship she had with her father, she realized that she had been doing just what she needed to do in order to survive and function. Once she was acknowledged and validated for doing what she needed to do, in the way she needed to do it, she was then able to acknowledge and express her conflicted emotions without fear of judgment or "being crazy."

Another woman said she never mourned or cried for her sister, whom she had loved dearly. Upon further reflection, she realized that she thought about her sister every day when she jogged and was inspired by her sister's life to continue teaching and helping others learn.

And some women (and men) tend to avoid their grief and pain by avoiding such emotions as much as possible. They stay busy, work twelve-hour days, drink excessively and/or use drugs. They jump from one relationship into another and/or become so focused on a particular goal or activity that they are, for a time, able to compartmentalize, push aside, numb out or ignore the feelings, thoughts and impacts of having someone die.

These are all natural reactions to pain, to not wanting to hurt. Usually, however, such reactions end up causing more complications and don't take away or change the pain of loss that remains.

I would ask that you take a moment to think about the women in your life. Think about their personalities, differences, relationships and families; how they interact with others; how they mourn and see themselves. Ask them which roles, lifestyles and behaviors they feel have been imposed or expected of them and which ones they have chosen or made their own.

They may be emotional, stoic, afraid, silent, loud, tearful, strong, confused, clueless, aware, insightful, isolated or social. They may be your partner, your sister, your mother, your grandmother, grandchild, aunt, colleague or friend.

I invite you to see and treat each of them as unique, creative human beings, who have the right, the power and the prerogative to deal with and react to life and death on their own terms.

MOTHER'S LAMENT

WHEN A CHILD DIES

"It's a girl!" "It's a boy!" "What a beautiful baby!"

The birth of a child is one of the most incredible moments in our lives. The joy and relief of holding a newborn after nine months of bodily transformations and hours of labor is, in many ways, beyond words. No less joy or fulfilment is felt at the time of adoption. Having an older child take your hand or a baby placed in your arms, is like a gift from heaven. As every parent is also aware, this newly added member of your family changes your life forever!

There's another event, of equal impact, that changes one's life forever, yet is seldom mentioned or acknowledged. There are no national days of recognition; no birthdays or ceremonies for the lost children; the children who have disappeared or died.

The death of a child (during pregnancy, at birth or later in life) is so horrendous, that we tend to ignore the thousands of women who have had such a shattering experience. Regardless of how the child is lost (miscarriage, abortion, stillbirth, disease, accident or kidnapping) the tentacles of grief invade the body and soul with an agony beyond description. Losing a child goes against all our beliefs about how the world "should' be. It makes no sense. It's not in the "natural" order of things.

When mothers (and/or fathers) try to put words to these life-changing events, they are often judged, avoided or bombarded with cliches. "It was only a fetus." "It's good you didn't know the child, then it would be harder." "You're young. You can always have another one." "Thank goodness you have other children." "Forget about it." "Try not to think about it." "Time will heal."

What parents who have lost a child want and need, are validation, loving presence and acknowledgment of their child's life and death. Ask about their loss; talk about their baby; find out how they're keeping the memory of that precious being alive. Respect their experience.

Our country honors dead people throughout the year. We have holiday after holiday for people most of us have never met, let alone known personally. Perhaps on this Mother's Day we can take the time to honor those we've known and loved who have died before us: those we've carried in our bodies and those who've carried us in theirs. Separation from our children or mothers does not mean we cannot continue that love, keep them in our hearts and lives and find room for their presence in our daily rituals and acts of remembrance.

This Mother's Day, I invite you to light a candle and place it by the picture of your loved one... acknowledging that bodies die, but the light of love shared never leaves. Or, plant a special tree or flower in your garden, as a memorial to your precious person. Take time to look through picture albums and quietly remember time spent with your mother or your child. Most of all - be gentle with yourself as you walk through the day.

WHEN MEN GRIEVE

"Be strong." "Bear up to pain." "Be sexually potent." "Provide for others." "Endure." "Don't give in." "Compete and win at all costs." "Be in control." "Remain rational, unemotional and logical." "Accomplish, achieve, perform." "Be assertive, in control and one step ahead of the next guy."

These are some of the messages given to young boys and men for over two thousand years. They've heard it from lovers, parents, families, friends, religions, governments, the media and other men since birth. Some of the messages of expected behavior are blatant and others are more subtle. Some are proclaimed orally or in print and others are non-verbal and observed by actions and deeds. "Don't cry." "Never, ever, express or convey fear, dependence, loneliness, emotion, weakness, passivity or insecurity."

It's only been in the last forty years, since the modern women's movement (in some areas of the world), that these cultural, familial and religious norms and expectations have been questioned, debated, challenged and/or changed.

After thousands of years and such a short span of freedom from such rigid conditioning, some men have chosen (consciously or unconsciously) to embrace these norms and continue the cycle. Others have revolted against them altogether and thrown out the positive attributes of such expectations, along with the negative. And others swagger back and forth between the past and the present, in a state of confusion, bewilderment and loss.

Regardless of how one lives their lives, when a man loses a loved one, by death or separation, they can be thrown into an unknown world of pain that casts their beliefs, personal expectations and accepted ways of being into an ocean of doubt, turmoil and isolation.

Loss causes an eruption of feelings, fears and thoughts that fly in the face of what it means to "be a man." Feelings of fear, anxiety, depression, emptiness, doubt, confusion, helplessness and indescribable pain assail our very concept and perception of who we are.

Efforts at avoiding, "toughing it out", controlling or "getting rid" of the pain of loss, only result in temporary relief, often at the expense of long-term health, and rarely change the reality of our condition. The pain of grief is one of the few kinds of pain in life that are best dealt with head-on, by doing something men are often taught to avoid. The pain of grief and mourning tend to change and heal with time and attention, when we can honestly acknowledge what we are feeling, thinking and believing and externalize such reactions in a positive, healthy environment and/or manner.

Men (and women) all experience the pain of grief and loss and both genders feel its impact in many of the same ways. What tends to be different about the sexes is how we talk about and verbalize such feelings and experiences. We filter them differently. Men often talk about the things we did for our loved one, how we took care of them, what we're "doing" now and what we "plan" to do in the future. We blame others or ourselves for something that did or didn't happen or something that could have been different; something that would have spared us the pain we are now experiencing. Our anger, guilt and reasoning; are ways we try to control and make sense of our grief and the situation it has put us in.

Though it is a generality and never true at all times, with all men or all women, men tend to speak "about", instead of "of" or "with." If I asked a gentleman how he's been "feeling" or what had been the "most difficult" about the loss of his wife, partner or parent, he might look at me as if I was speaking Russian. If, on the other hand, I questioned his "reactions" or asked him to tell me a story "about" the deceased, he would begin to take the road to the same valley of pain that a woman experiences, but gets there from a different route.

Ironically, men often seem to be more emotionally dependent on women for their sense of self, than the other way around. (Again, please remember that I am speaking in generalities and there are thousands of exceptions.) The women in a man's life are who he tends to share his most intimate needs, desires and fears with, as it is seldom safe or accepted to talk about such things with other men. Thus, when a female partner, friend or mother dies or leaves, men have nobody to whom they feel they can acceptably turn and their need for intimate human contact and emotional well-being is left in a desert of thirst for companionship, friendship, validation and/or physical contact.

Many men, though not all, also connect physical touch with sex, because it is one of the few occasions in their lives when they are permitted or expected to touch or be touched. To hug, kiss or embrace another man or woman, aside from the sexual act, is frowned upon and charged with a variety of expectations, judgments and fears. Thus, after the death of a loved one, men often do not know how, where or when it is acceptable or possible to have any human contact that is not sexual.

Luckily, there are people, men and women, who are willing and able to listen to men's lives and experiences surrounding grief and loss. There are places where a man can be held and touched emotionally and physically, without any sexual involvement or expectation of such. There are people within families, churches and communities that honor and respect our gender's differences without putting limits or expectations on what those differences can or should be.

If you or a man you care about, has experienced the loss of a loved one, give yourself or him the comfort, permission and love that all humans need, regardless of gender and provide the personal or community resources that can help the hurt change to healing and new beginnings.

GOOD GRIEF!

DON'T JUST SIT THERE, DO SOMETHING!

Mourning the loss of someone you love, adore, respect, hate, despise or have any combination of feelings towards takes time and attention, but you don't have to just sit there and take it.

Sometimes grief can cause such lethargy and exhaustion that it may seem impossible to "do" anything other than get through the day. The irony is that once you get moving, emoting or acting it usually increases your motivation, energy and health.

Once you have taken the time to acknowledge your loss (whatever it may be), feel its full impact and the changes it is causing in your life, you can then find ways to relieve, release, expel, create, explore and/or honor those feelings, sensations, thoughts and beliefs.

Though there are thousands of ways to release the pressure cooker of emotion and suffering that death can cause, here are a few possibilities. You can duplicate these actions in your own life or use them as a catalyst for your own unique creations and manifestations of grief. The only precaution is that you do them in a safe environment and/or with people you trust (where you don't have to censure yourself) and that they do not cause others or yourself harm.

Scream, wail, moan, sob, laugh hysterically, play music, sing, howl or cry out loud, in the shower, on the floor, into a pillow, at the beach, in the woods or with a trusted friend. After the death of her husband, a friend of mine said she would face the ocean and cry and scream for a few minutes every day and nobody could hear her.

Walk, run, swim, workout, hike, bicycle, dance, play or listen to music at least two to three times a week by yourself or with others. A man whose sister died in an automobile accident said running every day is what saved his life and made his loss bearable.

Breathing exercises, visualizations, relaxation, stretching, meditation, affirmations and yoga have all been shown to relieve stress, anxiety and positive endorphins to help the body heal. After my uncle committed suicide I found that deep breathing and yoga helped give me more energy when I felt sad or depressed.

Relax in a hot tub, hot bath, shower, sauna or sweat lodge and let the emotions seep from your pores and evaporate with the steam. A colleague whose mother had died suddenly said she attended numerous sweat ceremonies and found that she was transformed with new release and understanding each time.

Put together a collage, altar, memory book, picture frame, treasure box, video or audio tape/CD about the person who died. One family made a video of their father/husband before he died, which brought them great comfort in later years. A child I know routinely goes to the memory book she made after her mother's death.

Write, talk, pray, light a candle, burn incense or have a conversation with, too or about the person who has passed away. Many people find that talking to the deceased helps soften the effects of their physical absence and supports them in maintaining an ongoing (though different) relationship and connection with the person who has died.

Create a memorial, plant a tree, make a donation, volunteer, start an organization or dedicate an event, an action or your life to the loved one who has died. Some folks I know have created organizations or make a point of helping a neighbor or relative in honor of the person who died. To do so helps them keep the person's memory alive by embodying the attributes they admire and wish to hold onto in their own lives.

Don't let this list stop you from finding your own way to act, walk, crawl, run, jump or dance on your unique, individual journey of living with the reality of loss. You don't have to ignore or try to "get over" grief and morning by avoiding or suppressing it. Use it as a catalyst, as fertilizer, as and open door for change, growth and transformation. Don't just sit there, DO something!

INTIMACY AFTER LOSS

THE LAST THING ON MY MIND OR IS IT?

"My friends keep telling me I have to 'get out more' and meet somebody new." Jan stated. "Don't they realize it's the last thing on my mind?"

Jan's husband of thirty years died two months ago.

"My mother says I should stop thinking about Kathy and live in the present." Jamal said tearfully. "But I can't just turn her off."

Jamal's girlfriend, Kathy, died in a car accident on Thanksgiving Day twelve months earlier.

Steve says, "I'm not sure if this is right or not, but I met this lady and there might be something going on."

Steve's partner of fifteen years died after a long illness three months before meeting this woman.

"When is the right time?" Victoria asks. "How do I let myself get involved with anyone else without comparing them to Frank?"

Victoria's husband Frank died at age thirty-five, leaving her alone with two small children.

"I haven't gone out on a date in thirty years." Sally proclaimed.

"I have no idea where to begin. The thought of it terrifies me."

Sally's husband of thirty years died the previous year.

"This woman I've known for a long time asked me out," Paula says. "I'm afraid to get involved again. I'm afraid I'll forget Candace."

Paula's longtime friend and mate, Candace, died in her forties, after years of battling cancer.

"This may sound strange," Roberta explained. "But whenever I'm making love with Cliff, I wonder if Mark is watching us from somewhere and I feel guilty."

Mark died from a heart attack just two weeks before he and Roberta would have celebrated their ninth year of marriage.

"I've never loved anyone as much as I did Sylvia." Dale said. "I'll never find that kind of love again."

Sylvia and Dale had met when they were in high school. She died in his arms after struggling with lung disease for six years.

When is the right time? How do you know when or if you should get involved with someone again? Is it disrespectful or unacceptable to date, "go out with", "be involved" or "have a thing" for someone else after your loved one has died? What if you never want to be with anyone else again?

These are a few of the many questions that arise after a lover, partner and/or spouse has died. There are no steadfast rules or secret formulas to reassure someone who is experiencing and contemplating such thoughts and concerns about loving again, but there are some observations and suggestions that may provide some comfort and reassurance. Here are *some* of the replies I've given to those asking these painful, lonely and often conflicting questions.

There is no perfect or "right" time to have another relationship.

You may choose to never marry again and that's OK.

No matter who you join up with in the future, nor how deeply in love and involved that relationship becomes, **you will never forget the person you lost.**

Other people want you to "go out" again, not because you necessarily should or shouldn't, but because they wish to see you happy and they think another relationship will provide that kind of happiness and be the magic pill to "make you feel better."

Most **people who have experienced a good marriage or partnership have a natural desire,** at some point in their lives, **to repeat that experience.**

Look closely and honestly at your motivation for companionship.

How much of your wish to be with someone else is out of loneliness and need? What values or interests are you ignoring in order to "be with" someone else? Can the person you develop a new relationship with accept and understand that your deceased mate will always be part of who you are?

Loving another person and being loved by another, is a natural human need and desire. To do so shows no disrespect for the one that has died. There is plenty of room in our hearts to hold the loved one who died and love another. We don't have to throw one person out to make room for someone else.

You will never have an identical love or relationship with another, as you had with the person who died, but that doesn't mean you can't experience the same intensity or depth of connection with someone else. It won't be the same, but it can be just as profound and intimate.

Some people choose not to have another lover in their life and are perfectly happy. Others stay alone out of fear and some because of circumstances beyond their control.

Many times the questions surrounding when to or not to get involved with another come from our fear of losing someone again. When we have recently lost a loved one we are more aware than most of the reality of our limited lives and realize the fact that separation and pain will occur at some point in all relationships, either by one person choosing to leave or by death. We consciously and most often unconsciously, tell ourselves, "If I let myself love again and become intimate and attached to another, that person may leave or die as well. I don't want to experience that kind of pain again."

Such reactions are entirely understandable. We all try to protect ourselves to varying degrees and lengths from painful experiences, but to do so at *all* costs ends up being to costly. It cuts us off from other aspects of life. The question remains. "Is it better to have loved and lost, then never loved at all?" We must each find within ourselves when, how and/or if we choose to love again.

JUST AROUND THE CORNER

HOPE AND HEALING

I fell in love with Robin the first day we met. She was playing her role, as a recently admitted hospice patient, with great style and flair, while I lumbered through my part as the experienced "seasoned" social worker.

She wasn't nominated for an Academy Award and didn't give a damn about her looks. Her body looked like a skeleton with a layer of skin painted on with a thick brush. A blue and green scarf covered her almond-shaped, balding head. Her eyes sparkled like diamonds and her smile hung in the air like the Cheshire cat.

She had a warmth and graciousness that the worst ravages of metastatic breast cancer could not hide. Entering her small, low-income apartment by the sea, felt like entering a sanctuary or coming home for the holidays.

Her one-woman play about a terminal disease had about a two-year run.

She talked openly about dying, but more about living. She wasn't afraid of death, but she loved life. She loved her mother, her boyfriend, her family and friends. She loved music, art, beauty and nature. She was thirty-eight years old and she wanted to live until she was an old woman with grandchildren. She kept waiting for a new treatment, another remission, some kind of hope or miracle. It almost came twice.

An experimental trial with a new drug regime was supposed to be available through her HMO but kept getting put off, then delayed, eventually fizzling away into the land of false promises. Then came the dream of a cure with Angiostatin and similar therapies, which exploded across the media and public airwaves as "extremely hopeful cures for cancer tumors." Again she was told of some local trials and assured that she was eligible to participate, but this too seemed to fade into oblivion as time slipped by, leaving her to use whatever means she had at her disposal - blood transfusions, medications, hospitalization, intravenous therapy, diet, herbs, detoxification, prayer, meditation, visualization - she tried it all, but the cancer kept chipping away.

She went to the hospital for one final assault, then returned home. It was a glorious Indian Summer when I saw her for the last time. I knocked on her weathered door, heard her call out "Come in." and entered her tiny sunlit living room, which was also her bedroom, library and dining area.

Moving towards the head of her hospital bed, I saw that she'd been through the ringer and was losing ground fast. Her face was black, blue and yellow, as if she'd just been in a bar room brawl. Her skin was almost translucent, stretched over her frame like a sheet of white plastic. Her arms were as thin as straws and she struggled to breathe deeply. In spite of her frailty and obvious diminishing returns, her eyes still danced and she spoke vibrantly about life and healing.

"I hope my life made a difference." She said softly.

"You know it has." I reassured. "You've given such love."

"Yes, I guess so." She said and touched my cheek gently with her fingers. "That's been the best part."

"What's next?" I asked tentatively, wondering what she planned to do with her remaining days.

She turned away, looked out her large window and watched a mother and daughter lean against the cliffside railing, their hair blowing in the wind, the child laughing, screaming with delight. Without changing position, she replied. "I don't know. What do you think?"

Part of me wanted to run. My many years of listening and learning how to be present seemed to slip out the door. "I don't know." I said lamely. "Part of me doesn't want to believe this day has come." I followed her gaze, not really focusing on anything. My hopeless grasping continued. "I don't want you to die."

"Nice thought." She smiled, "but just a wee bit unrealistic." She rolled her eyes and grinned with amusement.

"Yeah." I blushed. "It's just... I don't know ..." I struggled to find the right words and then looked her way. "How do you let go of everything you've known with such dignity and grace?"

"I don't have any choice." She said without hesitation.

"I know we don't always have a choice over what happens to us." I blundered along. "But we have a choice in how we respond to what happens, don't we? If I was in your position, I'd be screaming and yelling to my last breath."

Without blinking, she reiterated. "Like I said, I don't have a choice. This is who I am."

Robin died two days later. She died like she lived, tenderly and peacefully. I, on the other hand, keep wailing away at the ravages of cancer, thinking I have more choices in life than are probable and hoping a cure for cancer is "just around the corner."

CONFLICT AFTER A DEATH IN THE FAMILY

People tend to react and relate to one another after a death in the family the same as they did before the death occurred. There are exceptions and occasionally someone will surprise us with their sudden outburst of anger, rejection or kindness.

It isn't necessary to drop hope altogether, but it can be helpful to remember to not live our lives with the expectation that someone we never got along with before a death will suddenly "see the light", make amends and become our best friend. If your stepfather never gave you the time of day before your mother died, he will probably continue to ignore you after she has passed on. If you have fought with your oldest sister most of your life, you will most likely do so after your father has died. If you and your brother always disagreed, he will probably want your older sibling who has died cremated and have a small memorial service for family only and you will want them buried, with an open casket and a large community celebration.

Carmen (not her real name) came to me in tears, saying she had been distraught and "beside myself" since her father's funeral. She said her older brother had "decided everything" without consulting her at all. He had started going through their father's home and getting rid of things that meant nothing to him, but the world to her. She was furious. She had confronted him several times and been dismissed as "emotional" and "irrational." She was wondering if legal action was necessary to stop him and if she had the energy to pursue such actions.

It hurt her to even be thinking of such things while grieving the father she loved so dearly. She had expected their family to grow closer and to support one another, not the opposite.

Frank (pseudonym) couldn't understand or deal with their adult son's anger when his wife died in a car accident. Frank had been in the same car and survived with only a scratch. His son and he had been having some difficult years before the accident and his wife had always spoken with their son every week. He had hoped they would be reconciled in their mutual time of grief, but instead, his son directed all his pain and anguish upon Frank. His son's reactions were "unbelievable" he said. "Here I am, trying to survive the worst time of my life, struggling with my own feelings of guilt, pain and loss and he heaps it on even more. I just don't have the energy to deal with him right now."

How we react at the time of death and how we grieve our losses can vary between night and day and are influenced by countless factors. A few of these factors are the age you and/or the deceased are at the time of their death; your unique connection and/or relationship to that person; and your familial, cultural, religious and societal expectations and conditioning. Is it any wonder that people from the same family can argue like cats and dogs over the funeral, blame one another for countless perceived injustices or even go to court over any money or belongings that remain?

"Should I make amends?" "Should I forget about it?" "When should I contact them again?" "Should I say something or not?" "Is there something I can do to get them to act differently?" "What will happen if I don't go there now and insist on my fair share?" "How can I avoid alienating them any further or being rejected and shut out?"

I wish I knew the answers to these questions. Like the journey of grief, there are a thousand paths, possibilities and reactions to conflict. The best I can do is provide a safe supportive environment in which people can describe their predicament without being judged. I can let them know about the journey of grief, how we all react differently, how we often project our own feelings, thoughts, pain and expectations onto others. I can let them express their pain, sadness, dismay, anger, guilt, remorse, rage and loneliness without trying to fix them or tell them to be or act differently. And I can ask questions to help them clarify their experience, put their situation into perspective and provide choices for further actions or decisions.

Some of the questions I have found helpful are:

If the funeral service was not as you wished, are there ways you can publicly or privately create rituals or memorials that are meaningful to you?

Why do you want to have further contact with this person?

What are you hoping will occur if you continue making efforts to understand and communicate with them?"

What was your relationship with this person like before the death occurred?

How important are the deceased person's things to you?

Is there an item or items that have special significance and meaning? If so, are they worth the anger, resentment or misunderstanding that may occur if you attempt to claim or ask for them?

How important is the present relationship to you now? Do you have the energy and/or time to "work on" or nurture the relationship that may or may not change?

What do you need most at this time in your life and how will you get it?"

Of course, we don't have to wait until someone dies before we ask these questions about our values, connections and the people in our lives. Perhaps today is a good time to think about those we want to be closer to and those we wish to release. Perhaps today is the day to make amends or tell someone we love how much they mean to us.

BRINGING DANIEL BACK TO LIFE

LOVE, INDEPENDENCE AND LOSS

(The following names circumstances and ages have been changed to protect privacy.)

"Stop the train! I want to get off!" Jean shouted.

Jean's son of forty-three years had died in a restaurant. He choked to death. He had survived a life of infinite struggle as he lived with Down's Syndrome and the isolation, stigma and cultural alienation he and his family had experienced daily.

"He was such a good soul." Jean continued, as tears streamed down her cheeks. "Of all the things to happen, why did it have to happen to him?"

Her son Daniel had become increasingly independent as he aged and was living in a group home in the Bay Area. He was working as a street cleaner during the day and enjoying a variety of social events with his living companions on his off-hours. Jean had visited him two days prior to his death, as she has done twice a week for the last fifteen years. She said she felt blessed, burdened and bonded with Daniel in a way only mothers of developmentally delayed children can know.

"Daniel was so in the moment." She said. "His smile was infectious." She looked down at her hands. "I know this may sound crazy, because people think folks like him aren't as aware of others, as they are of themselves, but Daniel," she grinned, "was always thinking about others. He could tell when someone was down. He'd give them a big bear hug and say, 'There, there.' She cried bittersweet tears. "He always said, 'I love love.' and would wait for you to say it. He wouldn't do anything else until you would say, 'I love love too.' back to him. He would just stand there waiting, no matter how long it took."

Jean had taken care of Daniel single-handedly for most of his life. Not long after Daniel was born his father moved away saying he couldn't live with an "abnormal" kid. In his home country, people made fun of kids like Daniel and would say they were cursed and had the evil eye. He blamed Jean and her background for the child's difference, telling her that her family must have done something very bad in the past.

So Jean, at age twenty-four, took on the already difficult and exhausting life of single-parenthood, combined with the complication of a child that would stay a child for much of his life.

No matter how much she loved him, the reality was that caring for Daniel was overwhelming and all-consuming. She seldom had any time to herself and finding support and child-care as he aged became increasingly difficult. Yet, she loved him like a mother loves an only child. Her identity, reason for living and self-image of who she was became increasingly ingrained with her son's life.

When she realized that his independence and happiness would be greatly enhanced if he learned to live on his own and separate from her, she was heartbroken.

Having him move to a group home for independent living, which was a forty-five-minute drive away, felt like having your ten-year-old go away for a weekend sleep-over and never coming home. She was petrified, anxious and relieved when he actually moved. She said she grieved a thousand deaths day after day and rarely allowed herself to enjoy the "freedom" of her drastically changed less-encumbered life.

"It took me years to grieve the loss of him as a boy, acknowledge him as a man and let go of my primary identity in the world as 'Daniel's Mom,'" Jean said, shifting her legs in the chair. "The last four years were wonderful. I had let go of so much, was doing things I'd always wanted to try and trusting that he was safe and happy. Then," she closed her eyes, as her head fell back, "then I get this call and he's gone. Just like that... no warning... no good-byes... no more 'I love love.'" She put her head in her hands and sobbed.

Later, after blowing her nose and wiping her eyes, she said, "Now I have to start all over again and I don't want to. It isn't supposed to be like this. I'm supposed to die first, not him." Her eyes met mine. "I want to get off. I want to just disappear."

She took a few moments of silence and then started telling me about her and Daniel; about all the funny, crazy, confusing, exciting, scary and unbelievable things he and they had done together. She told me about his temper, his sweetness and his frustrations with the world. She brought him to life again and again with her stories.

After another half-hour of hearing about Daniel, Jean placed her hand over her heart, closed her eyes and said, "He's not gone. I can feel him right here. I can hear him telling me to 'love love'."

IS THERE AN AFTERLIFE?

How we feel, believe or think about what happens to us after we die matters. It matters because our thoughts about the afterlife often affect how we react to and live in *the present.*

If one believes that their physical reality and what they see, feel and experience with their senses is all that exists, then the thought of its termination and our bodies decline *may* be frightening, if not downright terrifying.

If someone's faith tells them there is something that continues beyond the known physical realities of the world or takes them to a place of peace and happiness, they *may* be less inclined to fear their own mortality or that of others.

Both ideas and beliefs, that something continues beyond death or that nothing does, *may* also help us live more in the moment and appreciate the short, precarious lives we live or create continuing anxiety about how things are or where we would rather be.

The reason the word *may* is italicized, is because there is no omniscient law of nature, physics or human response that such beliefs in life after death or solely in the material world, causes *only* those stated or expected reactions. We are far more infinite than the stars in our complicated, yet simple, desire for understanding, comfort and reassurance about the unknown and what happens to us after we die.

When I was a teen, I used to believe strongly in reincarnation. At the time, it made sense. As I grew older my beliefs shifted from Yoga and Eastern traditions to Quaker activism and social responsibility. Then it changed again and again, from the Catholic Church to Judaism and from Eastern Buddhist belief in transgression and karma, to nature's continual recycling of all forms of matter, including human beings.

Whatever I was practising or following at the time, was my reality. Each exploration into the afterlife or spiritual nature of humanity gave me some answers and experiences I could hold onto, make sense of and say, "This is it! This is the truth! This is what happens!"

In my early work with hospice and later as a chaplain at the hospital, I met several people who had been clinically dead and revived or resuscitated. After hearing their stories and reading research that had been done with thousands of others who had had similar experiences around the world, I "knew" that some part of our consciousness or awareness as human beings (at least in the first few minutes) continues.

Most recently, after my acquaintances with several people whose cultural background and/or religious practices, have worshipped and spoken with deceased ancestors, I have begun to send blessings to and bring into the present, those in my family who have preceded me into death.

Because of my work as a grief counselor I have been granted the opportunity to explore the question of life after death with many people. Here are some of the answers, thoughts and beliefs that have been shared.

"Those who believe will find everlasting peace with Jesus and the Saints."

"God is the only answer. I know they are with God."

"My loved one always felt at home by the sea. When we scattered their ashes in the bay, it felt like he had been buried in his church."

"As a Tibetan Buddhist, I know my wife went through different Bardos (spiritual worlds) and gained enlightenment. She is such a compassionate loving being."

"When we're dead, we're just dead. There's nothing more and nothing less. That's why it's so important what we do while we are living."

"I believe there's a white light and the peace and joy are indescribable."

"The bible tells me there is heaven and hell. I hope I've lived a good life and go to heaven. I know my son is there waiting for me."

"My sister has come to me several times and told me she's alright. I have no doubt that she'll be there to meet me when it's my time."

"The Lord is the way, the truth and the light. I will be with my Lord Jesus."

"Maybe I'll see my parents when I die, but I don't know. I tend to believe that something better is waiting, that there's something more than this, but I couldn't say for sure."

"It's all chaos. There is no rhyme or reason. I have no idea what will happen after I die."

What's your experience been? What do you think happens after we die? What have you been told? What does your family believe? What does your religion teach you? What do scientists propose? How has the media portrayed the afterlife? Is death less frightening because of your beliefs? Do you think anybody "really" knows before they die what happens after we stop breathing? How do your belief or thoughts about life after death effect how you live your life now? Does it matter?

"THAT MUST BE SO DEPRESSING!"

WITNESSING LOSS FOR A LIVING

If someone at a party or social gathering asks me what I do for a living and I reply, "I'm a writer." They respond with enthusiastic glee and ask, "What have you written? Do you write fiction or non-fiction?" Or they say, "Really? I'm a writer too."

If that same person asks what my job is and I say, "I'm a grief counselor." There is a sullen silence and sometimes a physical backing away. Once they've gotten over their surprise they usually state glumly, "That must be depressing." or "I could never do that."

At that moment in the conversation, if they don't abruptly change the conversation and actually want to hear my reply, I tell them, "Yes, it can be depressing and it's not something everyone can or should do." Then I add, "It can also be filled with wonderful insight, changes, growth and humor."

As their facial expression changes from shock to disbelief, I explain. "I am privileged to be with people who have and are experiencing profound change in their lives and are re-evaluating their priorities and perceptions of the world, what they believe in and what they value. I get to intimately share their journey of grief and occasionally provide some objective observation, supportive words or simple kindness and compassion. Like the rest of life, we share profound sadness, confusion, frustration, anger, joy and laughter."

If they are still with me at this point I might say, "You're right. This isn't something everyone can do. It's not easy and it can be painful. It takes continuous self-reflection, energy and letting go of my own judgments, agendas and expectations. That is one of the primary reasons I have and continue doing this work.

There is nothing else I have ever done that requires such honesty, awareness and personal vigilance in order to get out of my ego and stop drifting to the past or present. The more clearly I see myself as I react to another, the more I can let go of what I see and be lovingly present for them at that moment, even if that moment is only a fraction of their lives.

I guess in some ways you could say work as a grief counselor is like meditation or prayer. You aren't very effective if you're on your own trip or think you can alleviate pain and change or save another human being. Changes do occur, pain is lessened and sometimes people feel like they've been saved, but it is they who have done the work – they and/or something beyond themselves. It's a very humbling job."

If the people I'm speaking to haven't fallen asleep by now, they either want to know more, tell me a story about an experience they have had with death or try to change the subject again by asking, "How interesting. What do you write about again?"

If I want to be mean and annoying, which I seldom do, I reply, "I write about losing children, parents, partners and siblings. I write about the death of pets, about funerals and loneliness. I write about…"

Before I can continue my litany of subjects, they've understandably excused themselves, gone to get another drink or suddenly remembered some urgent business at home.

My work can cause some anxiety and discomfort at parties

and it's not right for everyone, but I wouldn't pass up the chance to be so intimately connected to my fellow human beings for any other vocation in the world, except perhaps... a writer.

Dr. Gabriel Constans

About the Author

Over the last 45 years, my journey includes work with mental health at counseling centers, hospice, bereavement departments, hospitals, businesses, private practice, secondary schools, health and recovery centers, colleges, prisons, jails, and post-trauma programs in the U.S. and abroad.

My doctorate is in Death Education from The Union Institute and University. A Masters in Pastoral Counseling was from Beacon College and a Bachelor of Science in Human Relations and Organizational Behavior from the University of San Francisco.

There is much that I do not know, and it is in this not knowing that I continue to learn, and offer these experiences with grief and loss. Please contact me with any questions, concerns, insights or comments at: website: www.gogabriel.com.

Gabriel Constans

ALSO BY GABRIEL CONSTANS

A BRAVE YEAR - 52 Weeks Being Mindful

Like the rest of the body, it's good to exercise the mind. Daily exercise, and meditation, have been shown to increase health, by decreasing stress, which allows the body (and mind) to naturally release endorphins, relax and heighten awareness.

In this helpful book, Gabriel Constans leads fifty-two gentle and encouraging sessions planned to reconnect the body and mind. It takes courage, bravery, to honestly witness what we discover, inside and out, without turning away or getting caught in the content. It is a brave act to allow oneself to be still, if even for a moment, to look at one's present experience, face the world and grow stronger.

ISBN: 978-1739828127

Being Mindful: Exercises For Your Health

This toolkit of guided exercises by Dr. Gabriel Constans will help you look after your mind and body, whether you're dealing with peer pressure, anxiety, bereavement or school pressures. Whatever your worries, whatever you are going through, Gabriel will lead you through fifty-two gentle and practical sessions that will help you decrease stress, release endorphins, relax and reconnect with your mind and body.

This meditation guide can help you understand your situation and cope with your anxieties. It is a brave act to allow yourself to be still, if even for a moment, to look at your present experience, face the world and grow stronger. Let Dr. Gabriel Constans help you take control of your health and be brave!

ISBN: 978-1739323196

Papa's Favorite Smoothies:
Thirty-two healthy, delicious smoothie recipes everyone will love.

Join Gabriel (Papa), and the Smoothie Goddess, for the healthiest, most delicious, drink creations on the planet. Thirty-two recipes for any time of day or year. Lovingly tested and approved by children, teens and adults. Try them all, and discover which ones you want to savor again and again. Always cool, refreshing, and packed with nutritious ingredients and fabulous flavors.

Enjoy thirst quenching treats, such as, *The Blue Beauty* (blueberries, bananas, protein powder, yogurt, watermelon and nut cereal); *Pure Bliss* (milk, banana, cocoa powder, tofu, chocolate syrup and melted chocolate); *Best of Friends* (peanut butter, milk, banana, chocolate syrup and ginger); or *Super Strawberry* (strawberries, almond milk, pecans, plum, honey and vanilla extract).

Drinking Papa's Favorites may also invite the Smoothie Goddess to visit you in your dreams. If she does, send us a note about your dream. They are always magical!

ISBN: 978-1739323134